CROSBY, STILLS, NASH & YOUNG

ART DIRECTION/DESIGN: GARY BURDEN
PHOTOGRAPHY: JOEL BERNSTEIN [1ST DOUBLE PAGE SPREAD]
HENRY DILTZ [ALL OTHERS]
MANAGEMENT: ELLIOT ROBERTS/LOOKOUT MANAGEMENT
MUSIC ARRANGEMENTS: JOE ABBÉ
EDITOR: DAN FOX

WARNER BROS. MUSIC
488 Madison Avenue · New York, N. Y. 10022

Songs from

Crosby, Stills, Nash & Young
Dallas Taylor & Greg Reeves

Contents

complete contents on page 104

CARRY ON

Words and Music by
STEPHEN STILLS

6

ADDITIONAL VERSES

2. The sky is clearing and the night has cried enough
   The sun he comes, the world to soften up
   Rejoice, rejoice, we have no choice but to carry on.

3. The fortunes of fables are able to see the stars,
   Now witness the quickness with which we carry on
   To sing the blues, you've got to live the dues and Carry On.

   Girl, when I was on my own
   Chasing you down
   What was it made you run
   Tryin' your best just to get around
   The questions of a thousand dreams
   What you do and what you see
   Lover, can you talk to me?

TEACH YOUR CHILDREN

Words and Music by
GRAHAM NASH

Interlude

Coda

D.S. 𝄋

Verse 2. Teach Your Children well
Their father's hell
Will slowly go by
And feed them on your dreams
The one they picks
The one you'll know by.

(To Bridge and Interlude)

Verse 3. And you, of the tender years
Can't know the fears
That your elders grew by
And so please help them with your youth
They seek the truth
Before they can die.

Verse 4. Teach your parents well
Their children's hell
Will slowly go by
And feed them on your dreams
The one they picks
The one you'll know by.

(To Bridge and Coda)

HELPLESS

Words and Music by
NEIL YOUNG

ADDITIONAL VERSES

2. Blue, blue windows behind the stars,
   Yellow moon on the rise,
   Big birds flying across the sky,
   Throwing shadows on our eyes.

(To Bridge)

3. Repeat 2nd Verse

CUT MY HAIR

Words and Music by
DAVID CROSBY

*Guitarists: Tune low E to D.

ADDITIONAL VERSE

2. Must be because I had the flu for Christmas
   And I'm not feeling up to par
   It increases my paranoia
   Like lookin' in my mirror and seeing a police car
   But I'm not giving in an inch to fear
   'Cause I've promised myself this year
   I feel like I owe it to someone.

DÉJÀ VU

Words and Music by
DAVID CROSBY

down un-der you

Ah, __ ba, da,

ba-da, __ ba-da, __ ba-da, __ da,

Da, da, __ da, da, __ da,

4 + 20

Words and Music by
STEPHEN STILLS

Four And Twen-ty years_ a - go I come in - to this life, the son of a wo-man and a man who lived in strife. He was

tired,_____ of be - ing poor and he

was - n't in - to sell-in' door to door, And he

worked like the dev - il to be more.

Repeat D. C.
3 times Fine

ADDITIONAL VERSES

2. A different kind of poverty, now upsets me so
   Night after sleepless night, I walk the floor and want to know
   Why am I so alone, where is my woman,
   Can I bring her home? Have I driven her away?
   Is she gone?

3. Mornin' comes the sunrise, and I'm driven to my bed
   I see that it is empty, and there's devils in my head
   I embrace the many-colored beast, I grow weary of the torment
   Can there be no peace, and I find myself just wishin'
   That my life would simply cease.

OUR HOUSE

Words and Music by
GRAHAM NASH

*Note to Guitarists: The chord frames in this song represent only the basic harmonies.
We advise you to study the piano part for the beautiful bass and inner lines.

ADDITIONAL VERSE

2. Come to me now,
   And rest your head for just five minutes
   Everything is done
   Such a cozy room
   The windows are illuminated
   By the evening sunshine through them
   Fiery gems for you, only for you.

COUNTRY GIRL

Words and Music by
NEIL YOUNG

EVERYBODY I LOVE YOU

Words and Music by
STEPHEN STILLS and NEIL YOUNG

Ev - 'ry bod - y I Love_____ You,

Ev - 'ry bod - y I __ do. __

Though your heart is an an - chor,

I need your love to get __ through. ____

ADDITIONAL VERSE

When I tell you I love you
You can believe that it's true
Everybody I love you
Everybody I do.

CARRY ON

words and music by
STEPHEN STILLS

One morning I woke up and I knew you were really gone.
A new day, a new way,
And new eyes to see the dawn.
Gone you way
I'll go mine and carry on.

The sky is clearing and the night has cried enough
The sun he comes the world to soften up.
Rejoice, rejoice, we have no choice but to carry on.

The fortunes of fables are able to see the stars,
Now witness the quickness with which we carry on
To sing the blues, you've got to live the dues
And carry on.

Carry on love is coming,
Love is coming to us all.

Where are you going now my love?
Where will you be tomorrow?
Will you bring me happiness?
Will you bring me sorrow?
Are the questions of a thousand dreams
What you do and what you see
Lover, can you talk to me?

Girl, when I was on my own
Chasing you down
What was it made you run
Tryin' your best just to get around
The questions of a thousand dreams
What you do and what you see
Lover, can you talk to me?

TEACH YOUR CHILDREN

words and music by
GRAHAM NASH

You who are on the road
Must have a code that you can live by
And so become yourself
Because the past is just a good-bye.

Teach your children well
Their father's hell
Will slowly go by
And feed them on your dreams
The one they picks
The one you'll know by.

Don't you ever ask them why
If they told you, you will cry
So just look at them and sigh
And know they love you.

And you, of the tender years
Can't know the fears
That your elders grew by

And so please help them with your youth
They seek the truth
Before they can die.

Teach your parents well
Their children's hell
Will slowly go by
And feed them on your dreams
The one they picks
The one you'll know by.

Don't you ever ask them why
If they told you, you would cry
So just look at them and sigh
And know they love you.

HELPLESS

words and music by
NEIL YOUNG

There is a town in north Ontario,
With dream comfort memory to spare,
And in my mind I still need a place to go,
All my changes were there.

Blue, blue windows behind the stars,
Yellow moon on the rise
Big birds flying across the sky,
Throwing shadows on our eyes.

Leave us helpless, helpless, helpless,
Baby can you hear me now?
The chains are locked and tied across the door,
Baby, sing with me somehow.

Blue, blue windows behind the stars,
Yellow moon on the rise,
Big birds flying across the sky,
Throwing shadows on our eyes,
Leave us helpless, helpless, helpless . . .

CUT MY HAIR

words and music by
DAVID CROSBY

Almost cut my hair
It happened just the other day,
It's gettin' kind of long,
I could of said it was in my way, but I didn't
N' I wonder why I feel like letting my freak flag fly,
And I feel like I owe it to someone.

Must be because I had the flu for Christmas
And I'm not feeling up to par
It increases my paranoia
Like lookin' in my mirror and seeing a police car.
But I'm not giving in an inch to fear
'Cause I've promised myself this year
I feel like I owe it to someone.

When I fin'ly get myself together,
I'm gonna get down in that sunny southern weather
I'll find a place inside a laugh
Separate the wheat from the chaff
I feel like I owe it to someone.

DÉJÀ VU

words and music by
DAVID CROSBY

If I had ever been here before
I would probably know just what to do, don't you,
If I ever had been here before
On another time around the wheel,
I would prob'ly know just how to deal
With all of you.

For I feel like I been here before,
Feel like I been here before
And you know it makes me wonder what's goin' on,
Oh, under the ground, um, do ya know,
Don't you wonder, what's goin' on, down under you.

We have all been here before,
We have all been here before.
We have all been here before,
We have all been here before.

4 + 20

words and music by
STEPHEN STILLS

Four and twenty years ago, I come into this life
The son of a woman and a man who lived in strife
He was tired of being poor
And he wasn't into selling door to door
And he worked like the devil to be more.

A different kind of poverty now upsets me so
Night after sleepless night I walk the floor and want to know
Why am I so alone, where is my woman,
Can I bring her home? Have I driven her away? Is she gone?

Mornin' comes the sunrise and I'm driven to my bed
I see that it is empty and there's devils in my head
I embrace the many-colored beast, I grow weary of the torment
Can there be no peace, and I find myself just wishin'
That my life would simply cease.

OUR HOUSE

words and music by
GRAHAM NASH

I'll light the fire
You place the flowers in the vase that you bought today.
Staring at the fire for hours and hours
While I listen to you play your love songs all night long for me,
Only for me.

Come to me now,
And rest your head for just five minutes
Everything is done
Such a cozy room
The windows are illuminated by the evening sunshine through them
Only for you.

Our house is a very, very, very fine house
With two cats in the yard,
Life used to be so hard,
Now everything is easy, 'cause of you.
I'll light the fire
While you place the flowers in the vase that you bought today.

EVERYBODY I LOVE YOU

words and music by
STEPHEN STILLS and NEIL YOUNG

Know you've got to run,
Know you've got to hide,
Still there is a great light
Lingering deep within your eyes.

Open up, open up, baby let me in.
You expect for me to love you
When you hate yourself, my friend.
La, la, la, la, la, la,
La, la, la, la, la.

Ev'rybody I love you,
Ev'rybody I do
Though your heart is an anchor,
I need your love to get through.

When I tell you I love you
You can believe that it's true.
Everybody I love you,
Everybody I do.

COUNTRY GIRL

words and music by
NEIL YOUNG

Winding paths through tables and glass
First fall was new
Now watch the summer pass so close to you,
Too late to keep the change,
Too late to pay,
No time to stay the same
Too young to leave,

No pass out sign on the door set me thinking
Are waitresses paying the price of their winking?
While stars sit in bars and decide what they're drinking,
They drop by to die 'cause it's faster than sinking,
Too late to keep the change,
Too late to pay,
No time to stay the same,

Too late to keep the change,
Too late to pay,
No time to stay the same,
Too young to leave.

Find out that now was the answer to answers that you gave later,
She did the things that we both did before, now,
But who forgave her.
If I could stand to see her crying I would tell her not to care.
When she learns of all your lyin' will she join you there?

Country Girl I think you're pretty,
Got to make you understand,
Have no lovers in the city,
Let me be your country man.
Got to make you understand . . .

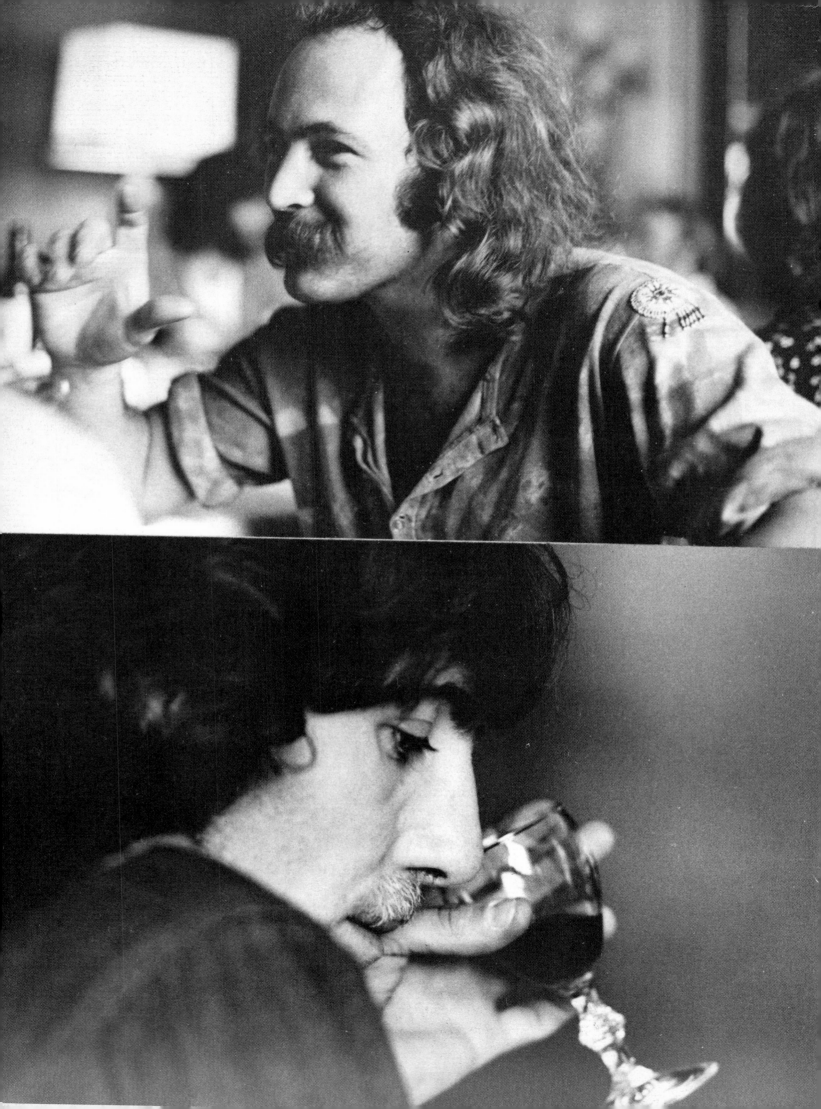

SONGS
FROM
CROSBY, STILLS & NASH

CONTENTS

SUITE: JUDY BLUE EYES
MARRAKESH EXPRESS
GUINNEVERE
YOU DON'T HAVE TO CRY
PRE-ROAD DOWNS

WOODEN SHIPS
LADY OF THE ISLAND
HELPLESSLY HOPING
LONG TIME
49 BYE-BYES

complete contents on page 104

LADY OF THE ISLAND

Words and Music by
GRAHAM NASH

PRE-ROAD DOWNS

Words and Music by
GRAHAM NASH

Moderate Rock

I have kissed __ you   so I'll miss __ you,   on the road __ I'll be
Felt de - ject - ed,   as ex - pect - ed,   you rejected all the

want - in' you. __   But I have __ you   'cause I love __ you
thoughts of work. __   So I'll pray, __ with   you, to stay __ with

and you have __ me 'cause you love me,   too, _____   Yeah!
me   forever, __   and we'll make it   work _____   Wo!

Felt for-sak - en, you'll a - wak - en to the joys —— of liv-in'
El - e - vat - ed, you're e - lat - ed, 'cause I waited— a year

hand in glove. —— And then I ___ will lend you my — will,
for you, _____ if you're think - in' what I'm think - in'

MARRAKESH EXPRESS

Words and Music by
GRAHAM NASH

SUITE: JUDY BLUE EYES

Words and Music by
STEPHEN STILLS

ADDITIONAL VERSES

2. Remember what we've said, and done, and felt about each other
   Oh babe, have mercy.
   Don't let the past remind us of what we are not now.
   I am not dreaming.
   I am yours, you are mine, you are what you are.
   And you make it hard - -

3. Something inside is telling me that
   I've got your secret. Are you still listening?
   Fear is the lock, and laughter the key to your heart.
   And I love you.
   I am yours, you are mine, you are what you are.
   And you make it hard,
   And you make it hard.

Fri - day eve - ning,___ Sun - day in the af - ter-noon,_
Tues - day morn-in'_____ Please be gone I'm tired of you._

What have you got to lose?_____

1.

2.
Can I tell it like it is?_ Lis-ten to me ba - by

It's my heart that's a suf-fer-ing, it's dy - in' and that's what I___ have to

lose.

I've got an an-swer___
Will you come see me___

I'm___ going to fly a - way,___
Thurs - days and Sat - ur - days?_

What have I got to

lose?___

1.   2.

Repeat 4 times

Do do do do do, do___ do do do do do, do do do do do, do___ do do do,

GUINNEVERE

Words and Music by
DAVID CROSBY

Guin-ne-vere   had   green   eyes,

68

D.S. 𝄋

ADDITIONAL VERSES

2. Guinnevere drew pentagrams like yours,
   Mi 'lady, like yours.
   Late at night when she thought that no one
   Was watching at all.
   On the wall.
   She shall be free.

   (To Bridge)

3. Guinnevere had golden hair, like yours,
   Mi 'lady, like yours.
   Streaming out when we'd ride through the warm wind
   Down by the bay, yesterday.
   Seagulls circle endlessly, I sing in silent harmony,
   We shall be free.

WOODEN SHIPS

Words and Music by
DAVID CROSBY and STEPHEN STILLS

If you smile at me I will

* Guitarists: Tune low E string to D.

ADDITIONAL VERSES

2. Horror grips us as we watch you die.
   All we can do is echo your anguished cries.
   Stare as all human feelings die.
   We are leaving, you don't need us.

3. Go take a sister, then, by the hand.
   Lead her away from this foreign land.
   Far Away, where we might laugh again.
   We are leaving, you don't need us.

HELPLESSLY HOPING

Words and Music by
STEPHEN STILLS

ADDITIONAL VERSES

2. Wordlessly watching he waits by the window and
   Wonders at the empty place inside
   Heartlessly helping himself to her bad dreams
   He worries, did he hear a good-bye? Or even hello?

3. Stand by the stairway, you'll see something
   Certain to tell you confusion has its cost.
   Love isn't lying, it's loose in a lady who lingers,
   Saying she is lost, and choking on hello.

LONG TIME

Words and Music by
DAVID CROSBY

ADDITIONAL VERSE

2. Speak out, you got to speak out against
the madness, you got to speak your mind,
if you dare.
But don't try to get yourself elected.
If you do you had better cut your hair.
'Cause it appears to be too long,
appears to be too long,
appears to be a long
Time, before the dawn.

49 BYE-BYES

Words and Music by
STEPHEN STILLS

YOU DON'T HAVE TO CRY

Words and Music by
STEPHEN STILLS

LADY OF THE ISLAND

words and music by
GRAHAM NASH

Holding you close, undisturbed before a fire,
The pressure in my chest when you breathe in my ear;
We both knew this would happen when you first appeared,
My Lady Of The Island.

The brownness of your body in the fireglow,
Except the places where the sun refused to go.
Our bodies were a perfect fit,
In afterglow we lay,
My Lady Of The Island.

Letting myself wander through the world inside your eyes,
You know I'd like to stay here until ev'ry tear runs dry.

My Lady Of The Island . . .

Wrapped around each other in the peeping sun,
Beams of sunshine light the stage, the red light's on.
I never want to finish what I've just begun with you,
My Lady Of The Island.

PRE-ROAD DOWNS

words and music by
GRAHAM NASH

I have kissed you, so I'll miss you,
On the road I'll be wantin' you.
But I have you 'cause I love you,
And you have me 'cause you love me, too. Yeah!

Felt forsaken, you'll awaken
To the joys of livin' hand in glove.
And then I will lend you my will,
And your days will be filled with love.

Don't run, the time approaches,
Hotels and midnight coaches,
Be sure to hide the roaches.

Felt dejected, as expected,
You rejected all the thoughts of work.
So I'll pray, with you,
To stay with me forever, and we'll make it work. Wo.

Elevated, you're elated,
'Cause I waited a year for you,
If you're thinkin' what I'm thinkin',
Then I'm gonna make my love to you, Wo.

Don't run, the time approaches,
Hotels and midnight coaches,
Be sure to hide the roaches.

MARRAKESH EXPRESS

words and music by
GRAHAM NASH

Looking at the world through the sunset in your eyes,
Traveling the train through clear Moroccan skies
Ducks, and pigs, and chickens call,
Animal carpet wall to wall
American ladies five foot tall in blue.

Sweeping cobwebs from the edges of my mind,
Had to get away to seek what we could find.
Hope the days that lie ahead
Bring us back to where they've led.
Listen to what's been said to you:

Wouldn't you know we're riding on the Marrakesh Express.
Wouldn't you know we're riding on the Marrakesh
Expressly taking me to Marrakesh.
All aboard the train,
All aboard the train!

I've been saving all my money just to take you there,
I smell the garden in your hair.

Take the train from Casablanca going south,
Blowing smoke rings from the corners of my mouth.
Colored cottons hang in the air,
Charming cobras in the square,
Striped djellebas we can wear at home.

Wouldn't you know we're riding on the Marrakesh Express.
Wouldn't you know you're riding on the Marrakesh Express
They're taking me to Marrakesh.

Wouldn't you know we're riding on the Marrakesh Express.
Wouldn't you know you're riding on the Marrakesh Express,
They're taking me to Marrakesh.

All on board the train,
All on board the train!
All on board!

SUITE: JUDY BLUE EYES

words and music by
STEPHEN STILLS

It's getting to the point where I'm no fun any more.
I am sorry.
Sometimes it hurts so badly I must cry out loud
I am lonely.
I am yours, you are mine,
You are what you are, you make it hard.

Remember what we've said, and done, and felt about each other
Oh babe, have mercy.
Don't let the past remind us of what we are not now.
I am not dreaming.
I am yours, you are mine, you are what you are.
And you make it hard.

Tearing yourself away from me now, you are free.
I am crying
This does not mean I don't love you, I do,
That's forever, yes and for always.
I am yours, you are mine,
You are what you are. You make it hard.

Something inside is telling me that
I've got your secret. Are you still listening?
Fear is the lock, and laughter the key to your heart.
And I love you.
I am yours, you are mine, you are what you are.
And you make it hard,
And you make it hard.

Friday evening, Sunday in the afternoon,
What have you got to lose?
Tuesday mornin', please be gone I'm tired of you.
What have you got to lose?

Can I tell it like it is?
Listen to me baby.
It's my heart that's a suffering, and that's what I have to lose.

I've got an answer, I'm going to fly away,
What have I got to lose?
Will you come to see me Thursdays and Saturdays?
What have you got to lose?

Chestnut brown canary, ruby throated sparrow,
Sing a song, don't be long, thrill me to the marrow.

Voices of the angels, ring around the moonlight,
Asking me, said she so free, how can you catch the sparrow?

Lacy lilting lyrics losing love lamenting,
Change my life, make it right,
Be my lady.

GUINNEVERE

words and music by
DAVID CROSBY

Guinnevere had green eyes like yours,
Mi'lady like yours.
When she'd walk down through the garden,
In the morning after it rained.
Peacocks wandered aimlessly underneath an orange tree.
Why can't she see me?

Guinnevere drew pentagrams like yours,
Mi'lady like yours.
Late at night when she thought that no one
Was watching at all
On the wall
She shall be free

As she turns her gaze down the slope to the harbor
Where I lay,
Anchored for a day.

Guinnevere had golden hair like yours,
Mi'lady, like yours.
Streaming out when we'd ride through the warm wind
Down by the bay, yesterday.
Seagulls circle endlessly, I sing in silent harmony,
We shall be free.

WOODEN SHIPS

words and music by
DAVID CROSBY and STEPHEN STILLS

If you smile at me, I will understand
'Cause that is something everybody everywhere does
In the same language.

I can see by your coat, my friend,
You're from the other side.
There's just one thing I've got to know,
Can you tell me please, who won?

Say, can I have some of your purple berries?
Yes, I've been eating them for six or seven weeks now,
Haven't got sick once.
Prob'ly keep us both alive.

Wooden ships on the water, very free,
Easy you know the way it's supposed to be.
Silver people on the shore line let us be.
Talkin' 'bout very free and easy.

Horror grips us as we watch you die,
All we can do is echo your anguished cries,
Stare as all human feelings die,
We are leaving, you don't need us.

Go take a sister, then, by the hand,
Lead her away from this foreign land
Far away, where we might laugh again.
We are leaving, you don't need us.

And it's a fair wind,
Blowin' warm out of the south
Over my shoulder.
Guess I'll set a course and go.

HELPLESSLY HOPING

words and music by
STEPHEN STILLS

Helplessly hoping, her harlequin hovers nearby,
Awaiting a word.
Gasping at glimpses of gentle true spirit
He runs, wishing he could fly,
Only to trip at the sound of good-bye.

Wordlessly watching he waits by the window and
Wonders at the empty place inside
Heartlessly helping himself to her bad dreams,
He worries, did he hear a good-bye? Or even hello?

They are one person,
They are two alone,
They are three together,
They are for each other.

Stand by the stairway, you'll see something
Certain to tell you confusion has its cost.
Love isn't lying, it's loose in a lady who lingers,
Saying she is lost, and choking on hello.

They are one person,
They are two alone,
They are three together,
They are for each other.

YOU DON'T HAVE TO CRY

words and music by
STEPHEN STILLS

In the mornin' when you rise
Do you think of me, and how you left me cryin'?
Are you thinkin' of telephones and managers,
And where you got to be at noon?

You are living a reality
I left years ago; it quite nearly killed me.
In the long run it will make you cry,
Make you crazy n' old before your time.

And the difference between you and me,
I won't argue right or wrong.
But I have time to cry, my baby.

You don't have to cry,
I said cry, my baby.
You don't have to cry, I said cry, my baby
You don't have to cry.

49 BYE-BYES

words and music by
STEPHEN STILLS

Forty nine reasons all in a line
All of them good ones, all of them lies.
Drifting with my lady, we're oldest of friends
Need a little work and there's fences to mend.

Steady girl, be my world.
Till the drifter come, now she's gone.
I let that man play his hand,
I let them go, how was I to know?
I'm down on my knees, nobody left to please.

Now it's over, they left in the spring.
Her and the drifter, lookin' for beautiful things.

Steady girl, be my world.
Till the drifter come, now she's gone.
I let that man play his hand,
I let them go, how was I to know?
I'm down on my knees, nobody left to please.
On my knees, feeling wrong.
My mind's gone, oh

Bye, bye, baby, bye, bye, baby,
Write, if you think of it, maybe.
Know I love you, go if it means that much to you.
Hey, but you can run, baby;
If the feeling's wrong before too long it's crazy.

And you're trapped, babe,
And you know that's not where it's at, babe.
You're just seein' things through a cat's eye, baby;
That's not my old lady.
Come on and tell me, baby, you better tell me baby,
Who do you, who do you love?

Time will tell us who is trying to sell us.
Bye, bye, baby,
Write if you think of it, maybe.
Hey, but you can run, baby.
If the feeling's wrong, before too long it's crazy.

And you'll try babe, and you'll know that's not where it's at babe.
You're just seein' things through a cat's eye, baby;
That's not my old lady.
Come and tell me, baby, you'd better tell me baby,
Who do you, who do you love?

LONG TIME

words and music by
DAVID CROSBY

It's been a long time comin'
It's goin' to be a long time gone.

And it appears to be a long, appears to be a long,
Appears to be a long time,
Yes, a long, long, long, long time
Before the dawn.

Turn, turn any corner.
Hear, you must hear what the people say,
You know there's something that's goin' on here,
That surely, surely, surely won't stand the light of day.

And it appears to be a long,
Appears to be a long,
Appears to be a long time,
Such a long, long, long, long time before the dawn.

Speak out, you got to speak out against
The madness, you got to speak your mind,
If you dare.
But don't try to get yourself elected.
If you do you had better cut your hair.

'Cause it appears to be too long,
Appears to be too long,
Appears to be a long time,
Before the dawn.

It's been a long time comin',
It's goin' to be a long time gone.
But you know, the darkest hour,
Always, always just before the dawn.

And it appears to be a long,
Appears to be a long,
Appears to be a long time,
Such a long, long, long, long time before the dawn.

COMPLETE CONTENTS